Salvatore Calabrese's

Sexy Cocktails

Salvatore Calabrese's

Sexy Cocktails

SALVATORE CALABRESE

ILLUSTRATIONS BY CONNY JUDE

STERLING PUBLISHING CO., INC.
New York

TO MY WIFE, SUE. Thanks, again!

Created by Lynn P. Bryan, The BookMaker, London
Designer: Rachel Gibson
Illustrations: Conny Jude (wnnyjude.com)

Library of Congress Cataloging-in-Publication Data
Sexy Cocktails / Salvatore Calabrese.
    p. cm.
  Includes index.
   ISBN 1-4027-1246-4
1. Cocktails. I. Title.
TX951.C2529 2004
641.8'74--dc22   2003063335

10 9 8 7 6 5 4 3 2 1

Published by Sterling Publishing Co., Inc.
387 Park Avenue South, New York, NY 10016
© 2004 by Salvatore Calabrese
Distributed in Canada by Sterling Publishing
C/o Canadian Manda Group, One Atlantic Avenue, Suite 105
Toronto, Ontario, Canada M6K 3E7
Distributed in Great Britain by Chrysalis Books Group PLC
The Chrysalis Building, Bramley Road, London W10 6SP, England
Distributed in Australia by Capricorn Link (Australia) Pty. Ltd.
P.O. Box 704, Windsor, NSW 2756, Australia

Sterling ISBN 1-4027-1246-4

Contents

Introduction

The music's playing softly in the background, the Flokati rug beckons as you slip from the soft-as-creamy-skin leather sofa to the floor... now, all you need is the seductive cocktail to make a dream come true. When another glass of champagne just won't do, what can you think of that will set the world on fire?

Try an *Angels' Delight*, closely followed by an *Angel's Kiss* or perhaps venture a little further with an *Angel's Tit* or is that too close for comfort? An *Italian Stallion* will aim to end up sipping *Seduction* and hope to be *Between the Sheets* indulging in a *Bosom Caresser*, and, a little risqué, *Bottoms Up*. Will she be *Dizzy* after a *Midnight Kiss* with *Moonlight*? After an *Orgasm* and even better, a *Screaming Multiple Orgasm*, will it be *Perfect Love*?

There's always been a sense of fun about cocktail names. This small, but perfectly formed, book is a light-hearted look at the relationship between sex and cocktails. Beautifully illustrated with specially commissioned drawings, it has been designed to whip any cocktail lover into raptures.

Throughout social history, the bar has been the place to flirt, and cocktails have hinted of sensuality. For instance, *Angel's Tit* was one of the most popular after-dinner cocktails during Prohibition. *Bosom Caresser* was the sensual idea of Harry Craddock at The Savoy Hotel's American Bar. *Between the Sheets* was created in the 1930s, as was the *Silk Stocking*.

It's not only the name that inspires sensuality; a cocktail's ingredients can be sensual, too. For instance,

sipping a creamy, chocolate-smooth cocktail is a sensual experience. You have to lick your lips, your palate reacts pleasurably to the texture and, as you will read later, certain foods are definitely aphrodisiacs. The difference between crèmes and creams is explained and, in the recipe section, these ingredients are mixed with enchanted spirits in the name of lust. Also featured is a list of Top Ten Tips to Successful Seduction to get you in the mood for love if you are not already!

Salut!

Salvatore Calabrese

Venus, recipe page 123.

Bar Essentials

Main glass types and sizes

Champagne flute	5oz/15cl
Cocktail	4oz/12cl
Highball	10oz/30cl
Liqueur	2oz to 3oz/6cl to 9cl
Old-fashioned	5oz to 6oz/15cl to18cl
Shot	2oz to 3oz/6cl to 9cl
Wine	4oz to 9oz/12cl to 27cl

Key to glass symbols in recipes

1   2   3   4   5   6   7   8   9   10

1 Cocktail   **2** Champagne flute   **3** Champagne coupe   **4** Highball
5 Old-fashioned   **6** Shot   **7** Wine   **8** Tumbler   **9** Goblet   **10** Heat-proof

Liquid essentials for sexy cocktails

Mixers
club soda
cola
ginger ale
mineral water (still
  and sparkling)

Syrups
gomme syrup
grenadine
Orgeat (almond)
vanilla syrup

Juices
cranberry
lime
lemon
mango
orange
pineapple
tomato
white and pink
  grapefruit

Extras
coconut cream
egg white
fresh gingerroot
ground black pepper
heavy (double)
  cream
salt
superfine (caster)
  sugar
Tabasco sauce
Worcestershire sauce

Tools

You need a shaker, mixing glass, sharp bar knife, barspoon, spirit measure, dash pourer, muddler, juicer, ice scoop, cocktail sticks, small grater for chocolate, and a zester.

Ice

Must be clean, fresh, and dry. Crush cubes in an ice-crusher or place cubes in a cloth and smash them with the end of a meat tenderizer. Do not use the ice remaining in a shaker for the next drink, because the ice will be broken and will retain the flavor of the previous drink.

Crèmes and creams

Crèmes and creams are not the same thing. A crème is a sweet and thick liqueur with sugar content. It adds smooth texture as well as sweetness, for example, crème de cacao and crème de cassis.

A cream is a combination of alcohol and dairy cream, for example, Bailey's Irish Cream.

Using a mixing glass

Cocktails whose ingredients mix easily and must be served chilled are made (built) in a mixing glass. Place about six ice cubes into the glass first and, using a barspoon, stir the ice around to chill the glass. Strain off any excess water. Add each ingredient and stir. Strain into a glass.

How to muddle

This is a simple action requiring strength in the wrist as you pulverize the fruit with the muddler to bring out its essence. Most of the fruit remains intact. Muddle directly in the bottom of the glass with a heavy base. Dice the fruit and place it in the glass or shaker. Add sugar (if stated) and/or a dash of mineral water (if stated).

Sexy Ingredients

What makes a wine, a spirit, or a liqueur sexy? Some spirits and liqueurs are far sexier than others. What defines this subtle ingredient, which makes a glass of champagne more desirable than a gin and tonic? Champagne has it all: sex in a sip. Centuries of word of mouth have made this the finest tool in the seduction kit. Wrap it in a glamorous bottle bag, add a silken bow and a billet doux, and you're sending out the right message. Love. Adoration. Forever.

Firstly, it's made by the French, and Frenchmen are known for their expertise as seducers, coming second only to the Italians... so it must be worth considering as a winner in the seduction stakes.

Secondly, it tastes sublime, as if virgins have stomped on the grapes of heaven and turned them into fine wine, the bubbles being a result of divine intervention. There's drama in the opening too. An expectation builds up as you twist the cork in your hand—will it spurt (oh, that erotic word) in a small fountain, or trickle out, accompanied by a puff of mist? Experienced seducers do it with just a twist, and a slight hiss accompanies the cork as it leaves the neck.

We are by nature sensual beings. We like to kiss and caress skin. Lick earlobes. Suck toes (preferably those soaked in champagne). The tongue is a sensual organ—an expert in taste and texture. Let it touch sharp, bitter, or unpleasant liquid and it will recoil in distaste.

Something that slips down the throat easily, making us slide the tongue slowly over both lips to capture every drop, is even more desirable. Such is the power of a liqueur.

Top Ten liqueurs, chosen for their texture and taste.

Bailey's Irish Cream
Cointreau
Grand Marnier
amaretto
limoncello
Tia Maria
sambuca
Galliano
crème de cacao
crème de menthe

Top Ten creamy cocktails

Angel's Tit
Blow Job
Bottom's Up
Cat's Whiskers
Chocolate Affair
Honeypie
Multiple Orgasm
Screaming Multiple Orgasm
Silk Stocking
Slippery Nipple

Bourbon will bring out the dark side of your sexual nature. Hot and strong-willed bourbon can make your heart beat faster.

Champagne is the king of all libido enlighteners. The finest effervescence will flash into your soul and remain there until a burst of euphoria bubbles over to make a night of sheer indulgence.

Cognac is the dominatrix of the spirit world. Strong-flavored, dark, and enticing, a crack of her leather-feathered whip will have you in ecstasy as she stimulates your taste buds into a fiery crescendo.

Gin is the innocent spirit whose destiny is to sin—no doubt about that. (Mother's ruin? Let's not restrict the ruin to just your Mum.)

Liqueurs are the leading liquids of lust. Sticky and sweet-tasting (remind you of anything?) smooth-talkers, easing the way.

Rum is the sex-kitten of the liquor world, all soft and mellow on the outside but hiding a punch to set the pulse vibrating.

Tequila is the spirit of the Latino salsa dancer, driving you to a wild frenzy with the slightest sip of the fiery liquid. Your lips will burn, your fingers tingle with each shot in the mouth, and Margarita will be just a sweet memory of the morn if you're not careful.

Vodka is the ice queen, chilled enough to freeze your desire until she wants it thawed out with a dash of another erotic liquid.

Whisky is what the Scottish drink when they're in the mood to roam the wilds. Two to three straight Scotches and you can only roll in the heather at dreamtime. They don't call it Scotch mist for nothing.

Chocolate

Once described as an erotic muse, chocolate is the food of love. Combine its flavor in a cocktail with cream and you have found the secret of seduction.

The flavor of chocolate is sublimely sensual. To me, it is an ingredient that helps me create a cocktail that will seduce with its silken touch on the tongue, and its allure in the glass. Cocktails with chocolate, in its original form or as a chocolate-flavored liqueur, have a beneficial effect on the sipper. Take my word for it. As actress Katherine Hepburn once said, "What you see before you, my friend, is the result of a lifetime of chocolate."

Chocolate stimulates the release of endorphins in the brain. Forget jogging! It also contains an amphetamine-like amino acid called phenylethylamine, a natural chemical that stimulates the central nervous system, causing that euphoric feeling that lovers get before and after. It's no wonder, then, that chocolate is associated with love.

Licorice

Black as black can be, leather-like licorice is darkly mysterious and, according to my female friends, rather like Dennis Haysberg: sex at a bite.

Licorice is as old as the sexual tricks it can awaken. Known as the elixir of life, its root contains small amounts of plant chemicals that stimulate sexual desire. Used by ancient civilizations such as the Chinese and Egyptians to increase sexual arousal and stamina, licorice is close to chocolate in the aphrodisiac stakes.

However, you do not have to eat it to gain the promised pleasures of this dark-haired beauty. Licorice has long been an essential ingredient in love potions. In the spirit world, extracts of licorice can be found in some classic liqueurs. Also, anise and star anise each have a flavor similar to that of licorice and a seductive background.

Anise is used as a sexual stimulant in many folk remedies, and is also used as a protection against evil. It is the oil garnered from anise seeds that's used to flavor Greek ouzo and the French-made pastis, Pernod, and anisette. It is also found in Benedictine.

There are several licorice-flavored liqueurs on the shelf. Usually they're served as an aperitif or a digestif. Here's the lowdown.

Pernod
An anise-based liqueur you can mix with water to turn it into a cloudy mist of dreams.

Pastis
It's licorice-flavored and favored as an aperitif, mixed with water.

Anisette
French mayhem in a liquid! It's a liqueur made from the anise seed.

Ouzo
A Greek tragedy version of an anise-flavored liqueur, it's good for mending a broken heart. Patrons pour the ouzo, dilute it with water, then stare at the opaque mixture in the glass for hours, wondering where it all went wrong.

Sambuca
A not-too-sweet liqueur with a hint of coffee in the flavor, created through an infusion of witch elder bush and licorice.

Tutti-Frutti

As one sensualist once remarked, "I always determine the sexual capabilities of a woman by the way she eats fruit." He was, of course, an Italian, a poet named Gabriele D'Annunzio, who lived in the late 19th century. He must have been a busy voyeur.

The apple, a crisp fruit, started it all in the Garden of Eden. Imagine that first bite! The juice dripping down the chin. It's no wonder the Apple Martini is sipped so frequently by so many.

Take the fig, one of my favorite fruits, and great in my creation, Fig Supreme. Both figs and grapes are connected with Dionysus, the god of wine and fertility. The very shape of them is erotic. Remember, it was the fig leaf that Adam used to cover his sexual parts in the Garden of Eden. Cut a fig in half and you are presented with the pink fleshy fruit, which looks just like female genitalia. Figs have been used in love potions since the Romans decided they needed help to get through a three-day-long orgy. And, the word fig is common sexual slang: nibbling a fig is, well, use your imagination!

The Banana

It's the shape that gets us all talking about this erotic fruit! And its taste: sweet, creamy, mushy, delectable. All the things that go with great sex. Full of healthy fiber and tryptophan—the amino acid that encourages relaxation—the banana was once forbidden to women in Hawaii because of its size and form! Maybe that's why the banana version is so popular as a classic fruit Daiquiri!

Top Ten Tips to Successful Seduction

1. Look her/him straight in the eye, full of desire. Don't let your eyes flit around the room.

2. Present your best profile, the one that makes you feel most comfortable.

3. Choose the name of the cocktail carefully so you sound as if you know what you are talking about.

4. As you drink, wet your lips naughtily.

5. Keep your cool even if she/he starts caressing your thigh.

6. Play with your hair, giving a signal that you are interested.

7. Be attentive to his or her needs, make sure he or she relaxes and is at ease.

8. Talk softly and slowly and with a smooth finish.

9. Don't rush it.

10. Remember, the male is the hunter, but it is the female who makes the choice.

Sexy Cocktail Recipes

Absolute Love

Pisang Ambon is based on the recipe of an old Indonesian liqueur made with exotic herbs and fruits.

1oz/3cl	**lemon vodka**
½oz/1.5cl	**Pisang Ambon liqueur**
½oz/1.5cl	**limoncello (Italian liqueur)**
½oz/1.5cl	**fresh lemon juice**
	bitter lemon
garnish	**slice of star fruit**

Pour all ingredients, except bitter lemon, into a shaker with ice. Shake. Strain into a highball filled with ice. Top up with bitter lemon. Add a stirrer and serve with a straw. Garnish with a slice of star fruit.

Adam and Eve

There is a bit of a fizzy finish to this herbal-based, slightly bitter cocktail.

2oz/6cl	**bourbon**
⅓oz/1cl	**Galliano**
4 dashes	**Angostura bitters**
dash	**gomme syrup**
	club soda

Fill an old-fashioned glass with ice. Add the gomme syrup, bitters, bourbon, and Galliano. Stir. Top up with soda. Stir.

Adults Only

The delicacy of passion-fruit flavor dominates this refreshing cocktail.

2oz/6cl	gin
⅔oz/2cl	limoncello (Italian liqueur)
1oz/3cl	passion-fruit purée
dash	passion-fruit syrup
garnish	twist of orange

Shake all ingredients with ice. Strain into a cocktail glass. Garnish with a twist of orange.

American Beauty

There's something extra delicious about this cocktail, dedicated to all American women.

⅔oz/2cl	brandy
⅔oz/2cl	extra-dry vermouth
⅔oz/2cl	fresh orange juice
½oz/1.5cl	ruby port
dash	white crème de menthe
dash	grenadine

Shake all ingredients with ice. Strain into a wine glass.

Angel Dream Special

One sip of this chocolate- and apple-flavored concoction, and you are sweet dreaming of angels.

1⅔oz/5cl	vodka
½oz/1.5cl	white crème de cacao
½oz/1.5cl	apple schnapps
⅔oz/2cl	heavy cream
garnish	grated nutmeg

Shake all ingredients with ice. Strain into a cocktail glass. Grate nutmeg over the top of the drink.

Angel Face

Here's a supremely gentle combination of sweet and sour flavors to warm even the coldest heart.

1oz/3cl	raspberry schnapps
6oz/18cl	hot chocolate
	whipped cream
garnish	grated chocolate

Pour the schnapps into a heat-proof mug. Add the chocolate and stir. Top with whipped cream. Add the garnish.

Angel Mine

Coffee and banana and cream—what more could anyone want for a subtle, sexy cocktail shot!

⅔oz/2cl	**Kahlua**
⅔oz/2cl	**banana liqueur**
⅔oz/2cl	**Bailey's Irish cream**

In a shot glass, layer the spirits in the above order.

Angelic Vision

After three of these, you might want to keep your visions to yourself.

1oz/3cl	**gin**
½oz/1.5cl	**fresh lemon juice**
dash	**grenadine**
	beer

Shake the first three ingredients over ice. Strain into a highball filled with ice. Top up with beer. Stir.

Angel's Tit

A quick and easy classic drink that leaves you with a sweet and smooth aftertaste.

1⅓oz/4cl	**maraschino liqueur**
⅔oz/2cl	**heavy cream**
garnish	**red maraschino cherry**

Pour the maraschino liquer into a shot or liqueur glass and float the cream on top. Garnish with a maraschino cherry in the middle of the creamy top.

Arise, My Love

If this doesn't do it for you, then nothing will.

½oz/1.5cl	**white crème de menthe**
	champagne

Dip the rim of the champagne flute into a saucer containing sugar soaked in green crème de menthe to make a green, crusty rim. Add the crème de menthe to the flute, then top up with champagne. Stir.

Bay of Passion

I used to row around the bay at Maiori on the Amalfi Coast to a secluded beach for an assignation. This drink is in memory of those great moments.

1oz/3cl	vodka
1oz/3cl	Passóa
4oz/12cl	cranberry juice
2oz/6cl	fresh grapefruit juice
garnish	red maraschino cherry

Shake all ingredients with ice. Strain into a highball filled with ice. Garnish with a maraschino cherry on the rim.

Between the Sheets

Created in the 1930s, the name of this cocktail has the perfect double meaning to excite cocktail drinkers.

1oz/3cl	brandy
1oz/3cl	Cointreau
1oz/3cl	light rum
dash	fresh lemon juice

Shake all ingredients with ice. Strain into a cocktail glass.

Big One

For those of you who have happy memories of being swept away in the surf...

⅔oz/2cl	banana liqueur
⅔oz/2cl	Bailey's Irish Cream
⅔oz/2cl	Grand Marnier

In a shot glass, layer the spirits in the above order. Gasp with pleasure.

Bikini Martini

Like its name, this is brief and to the point.

2oz/6cl	Plymouth gin
½oz/1.5cl	Bols Blue curaçao
1 wedge	lime
1 teaspoon	peach schnapps
garnish	orange rind

Squeeze the lime wedge into a chilled cocktail glass. Shake the remaining ingredients with ice. Strain into the glass. Add the garnish.

Black Dream

There's nothing quite like a dark and dreamy night for sipping creamy shooters with someone fascinating.

1oz/3cl	**black sambuca**
1oz/3cl	**Irish cream liqueur**

Pour the sambuca, then the Irish cream, over the back of a barspoon into a shot glass.

Black Lace

Always a sexy combination, however it is used.

2oz/6cl	**dark rum**
½oz/1.5cl	**Kahlua**
½oz/1.5cl	**Frangelico**
1 small	**espresso coffee**

Shake all ingredients with ice. Strain into a chilled cocktail glass.

Black Negligee

A richly flavored liqueur with a coffee and peppermint flavor.

1oz/3cl	**black sambuca**
1oz/3cl	**maraschino liqueur**
1oz/3cl	**green Chartreuse**

Pour all ingredients into a mixing glass with ice. Stir. Strain into a chilled cocktail glass.

Blow Job

1oz/3cl	**Bailey's Irish Cream**
½oz/1.5cl	**butterscotch schnapps**
½oz/1.5cl	**brown crème de cacao**
	whipped cream

Shake all ingredients with ice. Strain into a shot glass. Top up with whipped cream. Ideally, place on a flat surface, pick it up, and gulp it down.

Blue Passion

For those who are passionate about blue, this is the perfect cocktail—it's also strong and tangy.

1oz/3cl	**white rum**
1oz/3cl	**blue curaçao**
1oz/3cl	**fresh lime juice**
dash	**gomme syrup**

Pour all ingredients into a shaker with ice. Shake. Strain into a cocktail glass.

Bosom Caresser

A 1920s classic first made by Harry Craddock at the American Bar in London's Savoy Hotel. Sweet Madeira can be added to this recipe.

1⅓oz/4cl	**brandy**
⅔oz/2cl	**orange curaçao**
dash	**grenadine**
1	**free-range egg yolk**

Shake all ingredients with ice. Strain into a chilled cocktail or small wine glass.

Bosom Friend

It's likely you will never have too many of these in a lifetime—they're always good to lean on.

½oz/1.5cl	**amaretto**
½oz/1.5cl	**fresh peach purée**
½oz/1.5cl	**fresh orange juice**
½oz/1.5cl	**raspberry purée**
	champagne
garnish	**two raspberries on a cocktail stick**

Shake all ingredients, except champagne, with ice. Strain into a chilled champagne flute. Top up with champagne. Stir. Add the garnish.

Bottoms Up

One from the late 1940s. A rich and powerful drink to sip, and when you see the bottom of the glass, it's time to retire to bed. Van der Hum, a tangerine- and orange-flavored liqueur from South Africa, gives this drink a unique flavor.

1oz/3cl	**cognac**
⅔oz/2cl	**Van der Hum liqueur**
½oz/1.5cl	**heavy cream**
1	**free-range egg yolk**
dash	**grenadine**

Shake all ingredients with ice. Strain into a chilled cocktail glass.

Casanova

A sharp-tasting cocktail dedicated to the man who made his eternal reputation by seducing women.

1oz/3cl	**raspberry purée**
1oz/3cl	**clear apple juice**
2⅓oz/7cl	**champagne**
garnish	**two fresh raspberries**

Pour the raspberry purée into a chilled champagne flute. Add the apple juice and stir. Top up with champagne. Stir. Garnish with two fresh raspberries dropped in the drink.

Casanova's Ally

Here's a combination to make you feel alive each morning. Slurp it down in one gulp.

2oz/6cl	**fine cognac**
1	**raw free-range egg yolk**

Pour the egg yolk into a shot glass and add the cognac.

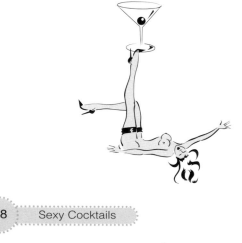

Cat's Whiskers

There are enough sweet and dreamy ingredients here for you to behave like the cat that got the cream.

2oz/6cl	dark rum
½oz/1.5cl	crème de cacao
2oz/6cl	coconut cream
1	banana
1	scoop vanilla ice cream

Blend all ingredients. Add a scoop of ice and blend again for a few seconds. Pour into a highball or colada glass filled with ice.

Chocolate Ace

The brandy brings a strength to the smoothness of the vanilla- and chocolate-flavored mixture. It's divine, and we've all done something forbidden, so sit back and sip.

1oz/3cl	cognac
1oz/3cl	crème de vanille (vanilla liqueur)
1oz/3cl	white crème de cacao
⅔oz/2cl	heavy cream
garnish	chocolate stick

Pour all ingredients into a shaker with ice. Shake. Strain into a cocktail glass and garnish with a chocolate stick.

Chocolate Affair

An intriguing combination of flavors that makes you want to lick your lips. Chocolate, almond, and coffee flavors and the kick of the cognac are bound by the cream.

1oz/3cl	chocolate liqueur
½oz/1.5cl	Tia Maria
½oz/1.5cl	cognac
½oz/1.5cl	amaretto
½oz/1.5cl	heavy cream
garnish	thin chocolate stick

Pour all ingredients into a shaker with ice. Shake. Strain into a cocktail glass. Garnish with a thin chocolate stick.

Cuban Passion

Anyone who has had the chance to go to Cuba will know what this kind of hot passion means.

2oz/6cl	white rum
1oz/3cl	passion-fruit juice
4oz/12cl	fresh orange juice
2 dashes	grenadine
garnish	lime wedge

Pour all ingredients into a shaker with ice. Shake. Strain into a highball filled with ice. Garnish with a lime wedge.

Deep Throat

A modern classic cocktail named after the classic film.

⅔oz/2cl	**Tia Maria**
⅔oz/2cl	**frozen vodka**
⅔oz/2cl	**heavy cream**

Build in exact order into a shot glass.

Desirable

A winning cocktail designed to bring out the desire in you.

1⅔oz/5cl	**lemon vodka**
½oz/1.5cl	**peach schnapps**
½oz/1.5cl	**cognac**
1⅔oz/5cl	**cranberry juice**
1⅔oz/5cl	**passion-fruit juice**
½ teaspoon	**clear honey**
garnish	**orange spiral**

Pour all ingredients into a shaker with ice. Shake well to infuse the honey. Strain into a cocktail glass. Garnish with an orange spiral.

Ecstasy Martini

The perfect eye-popping cocktail. Try it at home, and do not do anything serious after a few sips.

2oz/6cl	**frozen vodka**
½oz/1.5cl	**Cointreau**
½oz/1.5cl	**absinthe**
	sugar cube

Pour the vodka into a chilled cocktail glass. Add the Cointreau and stir. Lay absinthe over the top. Place the sugar cube on a teaspoon and soak with absinthe. Light the cube. Place over the cocktail so the absinthe catches fire for a few seconds (this burns off some of the alcohol). Extinguish the flames with a gentle breath. Drop the cube into the drink and stir gently. Sip and seduce.

Femme Fatale

Named after one of the most beautiful female movie stars I know!

1⅔oz/5cl	**vodka**
⅔oz/2cl	**crème de framboise (raspberry liqueur)**
½oz/1.5cl	**fresh lemon juice**
½oz/1.5cl	**fresh orange juice**
1 teaspoon	**clear honey**
handful	**fresh raspberries**
garnish	**two raspberries and a small sprig of mint**

Pour all ingredients into a shaker with ice. Shake vigorously to break down the raspberries. Strain into a cocktail glass. Garnish with two raspberries and a small sprig of mint on a cocktail stick laid across the glass.

First Crush

A cocktail designed to remind you of how it felt when you first encountered innocent love.

2oz/6cl	dark rum
2oz/6cl	fresh orange juice
2oz/6cl	passion-fruit juice
1oz/3cl	natural yogurt
half	a banana
1 teaspoon	clear honey
garnish	small slice of banana

Blend all ingredients until smooth. Add a scoop of crushed ice and blend again. Pour into a goblet. Garnish the rim. Serve with a straw.

First Fling

A cocktail not to be played with, but enjoyed to the hilt.

1oz/3cl	dark rum
½oz/1.5cl	Frangelico
½oz/1.5cl	apricot brandy
2oz/6cl	fresh orange juice
½oz/1.5cl	fresh lime juice
	dash grenadine
1	free-range egg yolk
garnish	slice of orange and a red maraschino cherry

Shake all ingredients with ice. Strain into a highball glass filled with ice. Garnish with fruit.

First Folly

O let that certain kind of sensual madness take me there time, and time and time again!

2oz/6cl	vanilla vodka
1oz/3cl	white crème de cacao
2 slices	fresh gingerroot
pinch	cinnamon

Shake all ingredients with ice. Strain into a chilled cocktail glass.

First Gasp

There's nothing more sensational than one of these.

⅔oz/2cl	sambuca
⅔oz/2cl	Bailey's Irish Cream
⅔oz/2cl	gold tequila

Layer the ingredients in the above order in a shot glass.

First Kiss

Here's a delicious mouthful for any time of the day, full of tart and citrus flavors to sigh for.

1oz/3cl	raspberry vodka
1oz/3cl	orange vodka
½oz/1.5cl	cranberry juice
½oz/1.5cl	orange juice
dash	Malibu rum

Shake all ingredients with ice. Strain into a chilled cocktail glass.

Forbidden Fruit

Why are all the exciting things in life forbidden? Here's one cocktail to give you a familiar thrill.

2oz/6cl	Tanquery 10 gin
1oz/3cl	fresh lime juice
handful	fresh raspberries
3 to 4	large fresh blackberries
garnish	a blackberry and a raspberry on a cocktail stick

Shake all ingredients with ice. Strain into an old-fashioned glass filled with ice. Add the garnish.

French Kiss

A double fizz and a burst of berries come together in this romantic combination of flavors in a flute.

1oz/3cl	raspberry purée
1oz/3cl	ginger beer
dash	apricot brandy
	champagne
garnish	fresh raspberry

Pour the raspberry purée, apricot brandy, and ginger beer into a champagne flute. Stir gently. Top up with champagne. Garnish with a fresh raspberry dropped in the drink.

French Knickers

A tart-tasting cocktail to suit its saucy name.

1oz/3cl	cachaça
handful	blackberries
1oz/3cl	fresh lime juice
2 teaspoons	superfine (caster) sugar
garnish	lime spiral

Shake all ingredients with ice. Strain into a cocktail glass. Add the spiral on the rim of the glass.

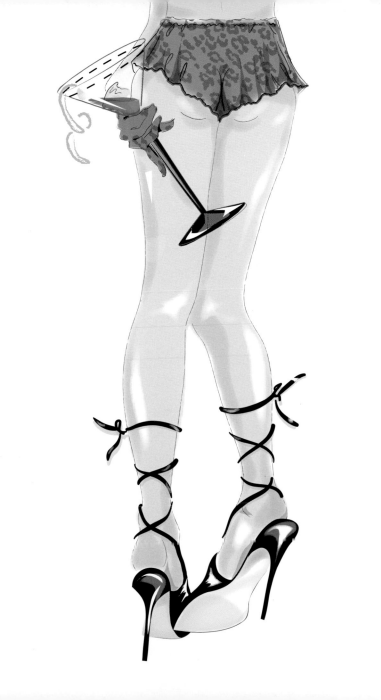

Funny Valentine

This cocktail has been known to stimulate more than the appetite for food.

1oz/3cl	**vodka**
1oz/3cl	**Passóa**
3oz/9cl	**cranberry juice**
3oz/9cl	**fresh orange juice**
garnish	**slice of orange and a maraschino cherry.**

Pour all ingredients into a shaker with ice. Shake. Strain into a highball filled with ice. Add the garnish.

Furtive Glance

It's late at night and you look at her; she looks at you... and that's it! How long can this go on? You smile.

2oz/6cl	**orange vodka**
½oz/1.5cl	**fresh pink grapefruit juice**
	dash Dubonnet
	dash Campari
garnish	**orange twist**

Shake all ingredients with ice. Strain into a chilled cocktail glass. Garnish with an orange twist.

Gallant Lover

An effervescent flavor combination that not only tastes superb, but also looks fabulous in the glass.

½oz/1.5cl	**peach schnapps**
1oz/3cl	**strawberry purée**
1oz/3cl	**pineapple juice**
	champagne
garnish	**1 strawberry**

Shake all ingredients, except champagne, with ice. Strain into a chilled champagne flute. Top up with champagne. Stir. Garnish with a strawberry on the rim.

Glenfiddich Fancy

The idea of a good whisky such as this being mixed with elderflower cordial has been known to bring a Scotsman out in a sweat. Try it and see what happens to you.

1⅔oz/5cl	**Glenfiddich 12-year-old whisky**
dash	**elderflower cordial**
garnish	**large slice of fresh ginger**

Fill an old-fashioned glass with crushed ice. Add the whisky. Set the slice of ginger on top of the drink.

Glamour Girl

Cool and sexy, this cocktail has the stamina of vodka, the sensual sweetness of Cointreau that rolls around your mouth, the sharp flavor of red currants, and the essence of ginger—whose healing power is renowned—and a final smooth hint of honey.

	1⅔oz/5cl	**Stolichnaya vodka**
	½oz/1.5cl	**Cointreau**
	2	**stalks red currants, destalked**
	2 to 3 slices	**gingerroot, peeled**
	½oz/1.5cl	**fresh lemon juice**
	½ teaspoon	**clear honey**
	garnish	**sprig red currants**

Muddle the ginger and the red currants in a shaker to release their flavors. Add the remaining ingredients and ice. Shake well. Strain into a champagne coupe. Garnish with a small sprig of red currants on the rim.

Go-go Girl

Spicy cinnamon flavor combines with the sweetness of peach to make a memorable cocktail.

	1oz/3cl	**cinnamon schnapps**
	1oz/3cl	**peach schnapps**
	1	**egg yolk**
	dash	**grenadine**

Shake all ingredients with ice. Strain into an old-fashioned glass.

Gorgeous Girl

Aren't they all gorgeous girls, whatever their age, size, or shape?

1oz/3cl	**spiced rum**
½oz/1.5cl	**apricot brandy**
2oz/6cl	**apple juice**
1oz/3cl	**cranberry juice**
1oz/3cl	**fresh lime juice**
	soda water

Shake all ingredients, except soda water, with ice. Strain into a highball filled with ice. Add soda water. Stir.

Go Wild

No excuses needed now that you have discovered the pleasure of this tempting cocktail. Let yourself go!

1oz/3cl	**vodka**
½oz/1.5cl	**Frangelico,**
dash	**soda**

Shake all ingredients, except soda, with ice. Strain into a shot glass. Top up with soda.

Great Head

Just make sure you get as good as you give!

	1oz/3cl	**Plymouth gin**
	1oz/3cl	**extra dry vermouth**
	½oz/1.5cl	**Cointreau**
	½oz/1.5cl	**apricot brandy**
	½oz/1.5cl	**peach schnapps**

Shake all ingredients with ice. Strain into a chilled cocktail glass.

Green Eyes

Baby, baby, don't make those eyes at me!

2oz/6cl	**gin**
½oz/1.5cl	**kümmel**
½oz/1.5cl	**kümmel green crème de menthe**
garnish	**green minted cherry**

Shake ingredients. Strain into a cocktail glass. Decorate with a green minted cherry.

Hard On

Here's a real man's cocktail, combining the aroma of coffee liqueur with the tough taste of bourbon.

1oz/3cl	**bourbon**
1oz/3cl	**Kahlua**
1oz/3cl	**amaretto**

Pour directly into an old-fashioned glass filled with rock-hard ice cubes. Stir. Serve with an ice cube in the mouth.

Honeypie

Dedicated to one of my guests who used to greet me with "Hi, honeypie."

1oz/3cl	white rum
1oz/3cl	cognac
1 teaspoon	clear honey
⅔oz/2cl	heavy cream
twist	orange zest
garnish	Cape gooseberry

Pour the rum and cognac into a mixing glass filled with ice. Stir. Strain into a cocktail glass. Shake the cream and honey sharply in a shaker with ice to blend them together. Float this mixture over a barspoon on top of the rum and cognac mixture. Squeeze a twist of orange zest (zest down-facing) to let a tear drop of orange flavor into the drink. Garnish with a Cape gooseberry on the side of the glass.

Hot Booty

Two delicious flavors—coffee and chocolate—combine to make this one hot number.

1oz/3cl	Sambuca
6oz/18cl	hot chocolate

Pour the sambuca into a heat-proof glass. Add the chocolate. Stir.

Hotshot Martini

With all these interesting flavor combinations, this cocktail will not disappoint even the most discerning palate.

2oz/6cl	**black-currant vodka**
½oz/1.5cl	**crème de cacao**
½ teaspoon	**Hershey's unsweetened cocoa powder**
½ teaspoon	**superfine (caster) sugar**
½oz/1.5cl	**heavy cream**

Shake all ingredients with ice. Strain into a chilled cocktail glass.

Huckster's Heaven

A cocktail you don't want to rush. Its effect unfolds slowly as the bubbles do their magic.

½oz/1.5cl	**crème de framboise (raspberry liqueur)**
½oz/1.5cl	**Cointreau**
1oz/3cl	**pink grapefruit juice**
	champagne

Pour all ingredients, except champagne, into a shaker with ice. Shake and strain into a champagne flute.
Add champagne.
Stir.

Ice Maiden

When you are faced with a soul that's as cold as ice, try tempting it to thaw with this cocktail.

2oz/6cl	light rum
1oz/3cl	apple juice
½oz/1.5cl	fresh lemon juice
dash	Campari
garnish	apple fan

Shake all ingredients with ice. Strain into an old-fashioned glass filled with ice. Add the garnish on the rim.

Idle Pleasure

Hidden under the flavor of peppermint is the hit of cognac and the stealth of absinthe/Pernod. Pleasure can only be idle after one of these.

1oz/3cl	cognac
½oz/1.5cl	Pernod or absinthe
½oz/1.5cl	Benedictine
1oz/3cl	heavy cream
dash	Orgeat syrup
dash	grenadine

Shake all ingredients with ice. Strain into a chilled cocktail glass.

Illicit Love

A cocktail designed to re-create the mood of the deep blue ocean.

2oz/6cl	spiced rum
½oz/1.5cl	amaretto
½oz/1.5cl	blue curaçao
3oz/9cl	pineapple juice
garnish	pineapple wedge

Shake all ingredients with ice. Strain into a highball filled with ice. Add the garnish on the rim of the glass.

Intimacy

A cocktail created to sip when the moment is intimate and you don't want to spoil it with anything less than a champagne fizz.

1oz/3cl	frozen vodka
1oz/3cl	white cranberry juice
1	sugar cube
	champagne
1 teaspoon	caviar on the side

Place the sugar cube in the champagne flute. Add the frozen vodka and cranberry juice, and top up with champagne. Stir. Serve with the caviar. Sip and swallow.

Intimate

You can share this apricot-flavored cocktail between just the two of you on a winter's eve.

1oz/3cl	**vodka**
1oz/3cl	**extra-dry vermouth**
1oz/3cl	**apricot brandy**
4	**dashes orange bitters**
garnish	**lemon twist**

Pour all ingredients into a shaker with ice. Shake. Strain into a cocktail glass. Garnish with a lemon twist.

Italian Lover

This is simply the best type to have, I am told!

2oz/6cl	**pear purée**
1oz/3cl	**raspberry liqueur**
	prosecco (Italian sparkling wine)

Add the pear purée and the raspberry liqueur to a chilled champagne flute. Gradually top up with prosecco. Stir.

Italian Stallion

Every sip will bring out the stallion in every Italian male! Guarantees satisfaction.

1⅔oz/5cl	amaretto
⅔oz/2cl	white crème de cacao
⅔oz/2cl	crème de noyeau
1oz/3cl	heavy cream

Pour all ingredients into a shaker with ice. Shake. Strain into an old-fashioned glass filled with ice.

Italian Thrill

This is a cocktail to savor the moment when a Ferrari wins the Grand Prix. Or you score first prize.

½oz/1.5cl	cognac
½oz/1.5cl	white crème de cacao
dash	vanilla extract
	champagne

Shake first three ingredients with ice. Strain into a champagne flute. Top up with champagne.

Japanese Geisha

A great combination of flavors ranging from sweet lychee liqueur to the gentle fizz of champagne makes this a commendable cocktail.

2oz/6cl	Bombay Sapphire gin
1 teaspoon	blue curaçao
1 teaspoon	Pisang Ambon
1 teaspoon	lychee liqueur
1 teaspoon	champagne

Shake all ingredients, except champagne, with ice. Strain into a champagne flute. Top up with champagne. Stir.

Jealous Lover

I am not sure I would give a jealous lover an opportunity to sip this unique cocktail because it is so delicious.

1⅓oz/4cl	Woodford Reserve
2 small	mint leaves
1 teaspoon	honey
4 dashes	orange bitters
½oz/1.5cl	Grand Marnier
garnish	mint leaf

Stir all the ingredients in a mixing glass with ice. Strain into a chilled cocktail glass. Add one fresh mint leaf to garnish.

King of the Night

Elderflower cordial is a deceptively intriguing ingredient. When combined with champagne, it positively zings!

1oz/3cl	cider brandy
1oz/3cl	fresh apple juice
dash	elderflower cordial
dash	fresh lemon juice
	champagne
garnish	thin apple slice

Shake all ingredients, except champagne, with ice. Strain into a chilled champagne flute. Add the garnish on the rim.

Kinky Kitten

This is a cocktail designed for no ordinary pussycat. Serve it to someone who likes the tartness of raspberry mixed with the smoothness of honey.

2oz/6cl	raspberry vodka
1oz/3cl	fresh lemon juice
1 teaspoon	clear honey
½oz/1.5cl	raspberry liqueur
garnish	a raspberry with a leaf of mint

Shake all ingredients with ice. Strain into a chilled cocktail glass. Add the garnish on a cocktail stick placed across the glass.

Kiss and Tell

There's so much of it going on these days, you'd better watch out!

1oz/3cl	**gin**
1oz/3cl	**medium sweet sherry**
1oz/3cl	**dry vermouth**
dash	**triple sec**
dash	**absinthe**

Shake all ingredients, except absinthe, with ice. Strain into a chilled cocktail glass and lay the absinthe over the top of the drink.

Kiss in the Dark

Perhaps this makes you feel adventurous in the romance stakes. Try one and feel the warmth!

2oz/6cl	**gin**
1oz/3cl	**cherry brandy**
1oz/3cl	**dry vermouth**
garnish	**maraschino cherry**

Pour all ingredients into a mixing glass with ice. Stir. Strain into a cocktail glass. Garnish with a maraschino cherry.

Kiss Me Quick

If you don't, then you might miss out.

1oz/3cl	**amaretto**
1oz/3cl	**raspberry vodka**
½oz/1.5cl	**raspberry syrup**
2 medium	**strawberries, hulled and diced**
1oz/3cl	**apple juice**

Shake all ingredients with ice. Strain into a chilled cocktail glass.

Knock Me Over

Ever been swept off your feet after a few cocktails? Try this and see what happens when you walk into a room.

2oz/6cl	lemon vodka
1oz/3cl	Drambuie
1oz/3cl	fresh lemon juice
dash	gomme syrup
garnish	lemon spiral

Shake all ingredients with ice. Strain into a chilled cocktail glass. Add the garnish on the rim.

Knockout

The heady taste of gin mixed with sweet and sour ingredients makes a powerful impact!

2oz/6cl	gin
½oz/1.5cl	fresh lime juice
½oz/1.5cl	apple sour liqueur
dash	Cointreau
garnish	lime wedge

Shake all ingredients with ice. Strain into a chilled cocktail glass. Add the garnish on a cocktail stick.

La Dolce Vita

Literally translated, this means "the good life"! After a taste of this, you will be in heaven.

1oz/3cl	vodka
4	seedless grapes
1 teaspoon	clear honey
	prosecco (Italian sparkling wine)

Muddle the grapes in a shaker. Add the vodka and honey. Shake. Strain into a champagne flute. Top up with prosecco. Stir gently.

Lady Love

A wonderful combination: a hint of mint and blackberry with an overlay of orange, held together by the port.

1oz/3cl	orange curaçao
1oz/3cl	ruby port
½oz/1.5cl	white crème de menthe
½oz/1.5cl	crème de mure

Shake all ingredients with ice. Strain into a cocktail glass.

Latin Lady

Tequila provides the fire in this true representation of a Latin lady's temperament.

2oz/6cl	**tequila**
½oz/1.5cl	**cointreau**
1oz/3cl	**pomegranate juice**
dash	**lemon juice**
garnish	**lemon twist**

Shake ingredients with ice. Strain into a chilled cocktail glass. Garnish with a twist of lemon.

Latin Lady-Killer

He's everywhere you look—handsome, beguiling, charming, and winning the glances!

2oz/6cl	**light rum**
½oz/1.5cl	**elderflower cordial**
½oz/1.5cl	**fresh lime juice**
½oz/1.5cl	**fresh orange juice**
dash	**Campari**
garnish	**sprig of fresh mint**

Shake all ingredients sharply with ice to break down the mint leaves. Strain into a chilled cocktail glass. Add the garnish.

Latin Lover

A mixture of cognac and Cointreau is guaranteed to bring tender emotions to the surface.

2oz/6cl	cognac
½oz/1.5cl	Cointreau
½oz/1.5cl	Chambord liqueur

Shake all ingredients with ice. Strain into a cocktail glass.

Latin Lust

When you are in the grip of lust, you need a strong cocktail to see you through the night.

2oz/6cl	gin
½oz/1.5cl	Pernod
½oz/1.5cl	crème de cassis (black-currant liqueur)
2oz/6cl	cranberry juice
2oz/6cl	fresh orange juice
garnish	stem of red currants

Pour all ingredients into a shaker with ice. Shake. Strain into a highball filled with ice. Garnish with a stem of red currants on the rim.

Leather & Lace

The tough and the delicate make an eye-catching combination, as does the taste of bourbon with raspberries.

2oz/6cl	bourbon
½oz/1.5cl	Campari
5oz/15cl	fresh orange juice
handful	fresh raspberries
2 dashes	gomme syrup
garnish	three raspberries and a mint leaf on a cocktail stick

Shake all ingredients sharply with ice to break down the raspberries. Strain into a highball filled with ice. Add the garnish.

Lip Smacker

The bitterness of the orange is guaranteed to get the taste buds salivating!

2oz/6cl	orange vodka
1oz/3cl	clear apple juice
1oz/3cl	fresh orange juice
dash	orange bitters
1oz/3cl	passion-fruit juice
garnish	orange twist

Pour all ingredients into a shaker with ice. Shake. Strain into an old-fashioned glass filled with ice. Garnish with an orange twist.

Ménage à Trois

Many a moment to be shared with this deep, rich cocktail. Sex in a glass.

2oz/6cl	mandarin vodka
½oz/1.5cl	Cointreau
½oz/1.5cl	Chambord liqueur
½oz/1.5cl	fresh lemon juice
dash	grenadine
juice	of quarter of an orange

Shake all ingredients with ice. Strain into an old-fashioned glass filled with ice. Quickly squeeze the orange quarter over the drink. Stir. Serve.

Midnight Temptation

The idea of these flavors together inspired me to create this harmony of apricot liqueur and coffee with port.

1oz/3cl	apricot brandy liqueur
⅔oz/2cl	ruby port
⅔oz/2cl	heavy cream
⅔oz/2cl	Kahlua

Pour the apricot brandy, port, and Kahlua into a shaker with ice. Shake. Strain into a cocktail glass. Gently float the cream on top.

Morning Glory

An intriguing cocktail of flavors that come together to create a glorious surprise—one to be relished.

1½oz/5cl	brandy
⅔oz/2cl	orange curaçao
⅔oz/2cl	fresh lemon juice
8 dashes	pastis (licorice-flavored liqueur)
4 dashes	Angostura bitters
garnish	twist of lemon

Pour all ingredients into a shaker filled with ice. Shake. Strain into a cocktail glass. Garnish with a twist of lemon.

Multiple Orgasm

Oh, the joy of this cocktail followed by the joy of great sex—in your dreams!

1oz/3cl	gold tequila
⅔oz/2cl	amaretto
⅔oz/2cl	coffee liqueur
⅔oz/2cl	Irish cream liqueur
1oz/3cl	heavy cream
2oz/6cl	milk

Pour all ingredients, except tequila, into a shaker with ice. Shake. Strain into a highball filled with ice. Float the heavy cream on top.

Naked New York

Someone's imagination carried them away! Drink as you watch reruns of the television series Naked City.

3oz/9cl	**vodka**
⅓oz/1cl	**dry vermouth**
few	**pitted green olives**
slice	**of blue cheese**

Pour vodka and vermouth into a mixing glass. Stir. Pour into a cocktail glass. Stuff the olives with blue cheese and drop each one in the drink.

Naked Waiter

This is something I have yet to come across in all my years as a bartender in many bars throughout the world.

1oz/3cl	**Pernod**
1oz/3cl	**Mandarine Napoléon liqueur**
2oz/6cl	**pineapple juice**
	bitter lemon

Pour all ingredients, except bitter lemon, into a highball filled with ice. Stir. Top up with bitter lemon. Stir.

Naked Waitress

I prefer this recipe to the previous one, as I am sure all guys would!

2oz/6cl	frozen vodka
dash	rose water
2 teaspoons	champagne
garnish	olive

Pour the vodka into a chilled cocktail glass. Add the rose water and stir. Float the champagne over the top. Serve with an olive.

Nanosecond Thrill

This is named after sex you'd prefer to forget.

2oz/6cl	vodka
1oz/3cl	cranberry juice
1oz/3cl	fresh lemon juice
1 teaspoon	clear honey
1	passion fruit

Scoop the flesh from the passion fruit and place in a shaker. Add the remaining ingredients and ice. Shake. Strain into an old-fashioned glass filled with crushed ice.

Nifty Joe

Rich berry flavors combined with citrus fruit turn this into a sharp cocktail for a sharp guy.

2oz/6cl	black-currant vodka
4oz/12cl	cranberry juice
½oz/1.5cl	fresh lime juice
	bitter lemon
garnish	lime wedge

Pour the vodka then the juices into a highball filled with ice. Stir. Top up with bitter lemon. Stir. Add the garnish.

Nymphomaniac

Here's another phenomenon I've yet to come across in all my experience.

2 oz/6cl	spiced rum
½oz/1.5cl	peach schnapps
½oz/1.5cl	Malibu

Shake all ingredients with ice. Strain into an old-fashioned glass with ice.

Nymphomaniac Nell

A delicious, fresh combination of fruits with the earthy taste of roaming bison in a glass.

	2oz/6cl	bison-grass vodka
	2oz/6cl	raspberry purée
	2oz/6cl	melon juice
	garnish	two raspberries and a mint leaf on a cocktail stick

Shake all ingredients with ice. Strain into an old-fashioned glass filled with ice. Add the garnish.

Open Arms

Here's a sweet and creamy flavored cocktail to make the mouth water.

	½oz/1.5cl	crème de banane
	½oz/1.5cl	white crème de cacao
	½oz/1.5cl	heavy (double) cream

Shake all ingredients with ice. Strain into a shot glass.

Orgasm

I discovered this recipe years ago when a lady walked into my bar and asked for an orgasm. I replied, "I am a little busy right now, but maybe later!" I did not know she meant a cocktail—I had not come across the recipe before! She laughed and gave me the recipe.

1oz/3cl	**Irish cream liqueur**
1oz/3cl	**Cointreau**
1oz/3cl	**heavy cream**

Shake all ingredients with ice. Strain into a cocktail glass

Oyster* Shooter

Here's my cocktail for stimulating your sexual appetite. (Do not substitute gin in this recipe because it will make you ill.)

1oz/3cl	**lemon vodka**
	cocktail sauce
½ teaspoon	**freshly grated horseradish**
dash	**Tabasco sauce**
1	**oyster**

Place the oyster and the cocktail, horseradish, and tabasco sauces in a shot glass. Add the vodka. Drink in one gulp. Have another.

* Just take a look at an oyster's form, texture, and aroma. No other seafood reminds us of the sexual organ as does the oyster from the deep. There is proof that the constituents of an oyster enhance sexual performance. Number one enhancer: zinc, the one mineral that's great for male testerone levels and hence virility. In other words, oysters are sex in a shell. The French lead the world in consumption of oysters, and look at their sexual reputation!

Passion Martini

More than a night's passion will result from a sip of this.

2oz/6cl	passion-fruit vodka
½oz/1.5cl	Passóa liqueur
1	passion fruit

Scoop the flesh out of the passion fruit and place in a shaker with ice. Add liquid ingredients and shake well. Strain into a chilled cocktail glass.

Penny's Passion

Dedicated to a friend whose passion for life often carries her away into another realm.

2oz/6cl	vodka
2⅓oz/7cl	apple juice
1oz/3cl	fresh lime juice
1 teaspoon	superfine (caster) sugar
1⅔oz/5cl	passion-fruit juice

Pour all ingredients into a shaker with ice. Shake. Strain into a highball filled with crushed ice. Scoop out the pulp of the passion fruit and lay it on top of the drink: it gives it a piquant aroma. Serve with a stirrer.

Pep Talk

Pepper is good for the digestion, and this cocktail will make you feel wonderful, ready for an after-dinner romp.

2oz/6cl	**vodka**
½oz/1.5cl	**Grand Marnier**
½oz/1.5cl	**raspberry liqueur**
1 teaspoon	**pink peppercorns (whole)**

Shake all ingredients vigorously with ice. Strain into a chilled cocktail glass. The peppercorns will float to the top, creating an attractive layer on top of the drink. Each sip will be a mixture of sweet and spicy flavors.

Perfect Love

There can be no half-measures with a rich and fruity taste sensation such as this.

2oz/6cl	**red-currant vodka**
½oz/1.5cl	**crème de cassis**
½oz/1.5cl	**fresh lemon juice**
dash	**gomme syrup**
garnish	**orange twist**

Shake all ingredients with ice. Strain into a chilled cocktail glass. Add the garnish on the rim of the glass.

Playmate

All of the different flavors play with the taste buds in a saucy way.

⅔oz/2cl	apricot brandy
⅔oz/2cl	brandy
⅔oz/2cl	Grand Marnier
⅔oz/2cl	fresh orange juice
1 teaspoon	egg, beaten
4 dashes	Angostura bitters
garnish	orange twist

Shake all ingredients with ice. Strain into a cocktail glass. Garnish with an orange twist.

Play with Me

Rum and ginger beer provide the spice of life in this cocktail!

2oz/6cl	spiced rum
1oz/3cl	fresh lime juice
½oz/1.5cl	Cointreau
	ginger beer
garnish	lime wedge

Shake all ingredients, except ginger beer, with ice. Strain into a highball filled with ice. Top up with ginger beer. Stir. Add the garnish.

Pure and Edible

There are many layers to explore in this rich cocktail.

2oz/6cl	**golden rum**
1oz/3cl	**Kahlua**
2 teaspoons	**cocoa powder**
1	**espresso coffee**
garnish	**three coffee beans**

Shake all ingredients with ice. Strain into a chilled cocktail glass. Add the three beans on top of the drink.

Pure Delight

⅔oz/2cl	**chambord**
½oz/1.5cl	**peach schnapps**
½oz/1.5cl	**black chocolate liqueur**
garnish	**1 strawberry and 2 small mint leaves**

Mix the chambord and peach schnapps in a mixing glass filled with ice. Strain into a chilled cocktail glass. Float the liqueur over the top. Add the garnish on the rim.

Pure Ecstasy

For those of you who want to experience this state of mind and body, try this combination of stimulating liquors.

2oz/6cl	**frozen vodka**
½oz/1.5cl	**absinthe/Pernod**
½oz/1.5cl	**champagne**
1	**sugar cube**

Pour the frozen vodka into a chilled cocktail glass. Add the champagne on top and stir. Soak the sugar cube in the absinthe/Pernod and drop into the drink. Serve.

Pure Essence of Love

A delightful long drink, with a peach flavor, to make you purr all night long.

2oz/6cl	**Campari**
1oz/3cl	**peach brandy**
	bitter lemon

Pour the first two ingredients into a shaker filled with ice. Shake. Strain into a highball filled with ice. Top up with bitter lemon. Stir.

Pure Fetish

If you have a penchant for kinkiness in any form, then this is your cocktail.

1oz/3cl	vodka
1oz/3cl	peach schnapps
2oz/6cl	cranberry juice
2oz/6cl	fresh orange juice
garnish	wedge of lime

Pour all ingredients into a shaker with ice. Shake. Strain into an old-fashioned glass filled with ice. Garnish with a wedge of lime.

Pure Thrill

A pale beige color, this is a creamy mouthful to enjoy late at night.

1oz/3cl	coffee liqueur
½oz/1.5cl	amaretto
	Guiness

Build this cocktail in a tumbler or beer glass. Add the coffee liqueur, then the amaretto, then top up with Guiness, pouring it in slowly. Stir. Serve.

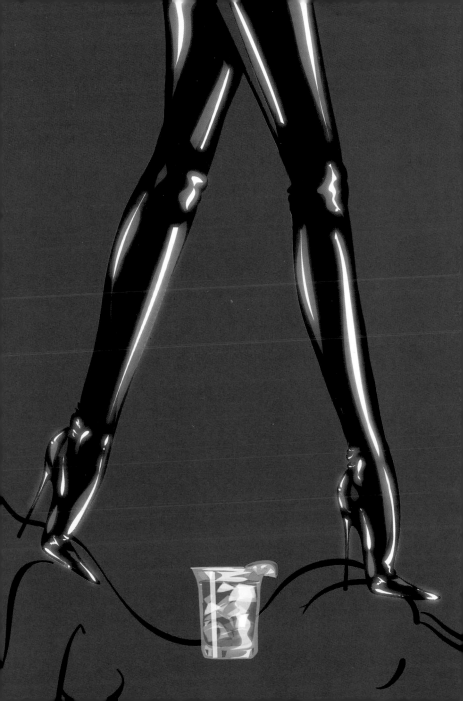

Pussycat

1⅔oz/5cl	bourbon
1oz/3cl	fresh lime juice
2oz/6cl	fresh orange juice
⅓oz/1cl	grenadine
⅔oz/2cl	gomme syrup

Pour all ingredients into a shaker with ice. Shake. Strain into an old-fashioned glass filled with ice.

Raver

Galliano and cream make the heart beat faster, especially when combined with espresso coffee!

1oz/3cl	Galliano
1oz/3cl	brown crème de cacao
1oz/3cl	heavy cream
1	espresso coffee
garnish	shaved chocolate

Shake all ingredients, except cream, with ice. Strain into a chilled cocktail glass. Float the cream over the top. Garnish with shaved chocolate over the cream.

Ready for Bed

A layered cocktail that brings more meaning to the words "Ready for bed?"

½oz/1.5cl	**Kahlua**
½oz/1.5cl	**amaretto**
½oz/1.5cl	**vanilla-infused rum**

Layer the spirits in the order of the recipe in a shot glass.

Red Hot

Creamy hot chocolate and dark rum! Whipped cream! When it's hot, it's hot!

1oz/3cl	**dark rum**
1oz/3cl	**Frangelico**
6oz/18cl	**hot chocolate**
	whipped cream
garnish	**chocolate shavings**

Combine the spirits in a heat-proof coffee mug. Fill with hot chocolate. Stir. Top with whipped cream and add the garnish.

Red-Hot Lover

The spicy flavor of pepper mixed with vodka guarantees a flavorful moment or more.

2oz/6cl	**pepper vodka**
½oz/1.5cl	**fresh lime juice**
½oz/1.5cl	**grenadine**

Shake all ingredients with ice. Strain into an old-fashioned glass filled with ice. Serve.

Red Lips

Innocence is banished the moment red lips make their appearance.

1oz/3cl	white rum
1oz/3cl	white crème de cacao
1oz/3cl	heavy cream
2 dashes	grenadine

Shake all ingredients with ice. Strain into a chilled cocktail glass.

Rude Cosmopolitan

A tequila-based Cosmopolitan (usually made with vodka). This is an interesting version.

1⅔oz/5cl	gold tequila
½oz/1.5cl	triple sec/Cointreau
1oz/3cl	cranberry juice
½oz/1.5cl	fresh lime juice
garnish	orange twist

Pour all ingredients into a shaker with ice. Shake. Strain into a cocktail glass. Garnish with an orange twist.

Screaming Multiple Orgasm

No, it's not just an urban myth—they do exist! Ask any woman.

1oz/3cl	**Bailey's Irish Cream**
1oz/3cl	**Cointreau**
½oz/1.5cl	**Galliano**
1oz/3cl	**heavy cream**

Build over ice in an old-fashioned glass and stir.

Seduction

A great cocktail that will work its magic when time is short and you need to make a hit.

2oz/6cl	**cachaça**
½oz/1.5cl	**Midori**
2oz/6cl	**cream of coconut**
5oz/15cl	**pineapple juice**
garnish	**pineapple wedge**

Blend all ingredients with crushed ice. Pour into a highball glass. Add the garnish on top of the drink.

Sex at Last

When the moment is right, here's the cocktail to ease the moment.

½oz/1.5cl	**Tia Maria**
½oz/1.5cl	**dark rum**
1⅔oz/5cl	**pineapple juice**
½oz/1.5cl	**Barbadian rum**

Shake together the first three ingredients with ice. Strain into a cocktail glass. Float the Barbadian rum over the top of the liquid.

Sex by the Pool

Let's hope it will be as good as sex anywhere else!

2oz/6cl	**gin**
½oz/1.5cl	**blue curaçao**
1oz/3cl	**blonde Dubonnet**
½oz/1.5cl	**fresh lemon juice**
dash	**gomme syrup**
dash	**white cranberry juice**

Shake all ingredients with ice. Strain into a chilled cocktail glass.

Sex on the Beach

There are many versions of this drink around today. The popular version is printed below.

1oz/3cl	vodka
½oz/1.5cl	peach schnapps
½oz/1.5cl	Chambord liqueur
1⅔oz/5cl	fresh orange juice
1⅔oz/5cl	cranberry juice
garnish	slice of lime

Pour all ingredients into a shaker with ice. Shake. Strain into a highball filled with ice. Add the garnish.

Sex on the Lounger

More tutti-frutti for frolicking by the outdoor pool, or maybe you just want to stay in the poolhouse.

1oz/3cl	Bacardi lemon
½oz/1.5cl	blue curaçao
½oz/1.5cl	fresh lemon juice
1oz/3cl	pineapple juice
1oz/3cl	fresh orange juice

Shake all ingredients with ice. Strain into a chilled cocktail glass.

Sex on the Slopes

Here's a hot cocktail for when it's cool, cool, cool out there.

1oz/3cl	dark rum
½oz/1.5cl	Southern Comfort
6 oz/18cl	iced tea
dash	fresh lemon juice
garnish	slice of lemon

Build over ice in a highball. Stir. Garnish with a slice of lemon.

Sex with You

And maybe somebody else later if I have the stamina.

2oz/6oz	tequila
1oz/3cl	fresh lime juice
1oz/3cl	white cranberry juice
dash	cherry syrup
garnish	lime wedge

Shake all ingredients with ice.
Strain into an old-fashioned glass
filled with ice. Add the garnish.

Silk and Sin

Two of my favorite things together in a cocktail.

2oz/6cl	**Scotch**
1oz/3cl	**Advocaat**
2oz/6cl	**milk**

Shake all ingredients with ice. Strain into an old-fashioned glass filled with ice. Shudder at the sheer chilled thrill of it.

Silk Stocking

One that brings back memories of the past, this has a creamy chocolate and cinnamon flavor.

1⅔oz/5cl	**silver tequila**
⅔oz/2cl	**white crème de cacao**
1oz/3cl	**heavy cream**
dash	**grenadine**
wedge	**lime**

Rub a wedge of lime around the rim of a cocktail glass. Dip it into a saucer full of grated cinnamon. Pour all ingredients into a shaker with ice. Shake. Strain into a cocktail glass.

Sit on My Face

And tell me that you love me—isn't that the way the song goes?

½oz/1.5cl	blackberry brandy
½oz/1.5cl	amaretto
½oz/1.5cl	triple sec
½oz/1.5cl	lime juice

Shake all ingredients with ice. Strain into a chilled shot glass.

Slippery Dick

Not to be confused with Tricky Dicky, a popular nickname for ex-President Nixon.

1oz/3cl	peppermint schnapps
1oz/3cl	amaretto

Layer in a shot glass. Lick the glass afterward.

Slippery Nipple

This sensual shooter has gained a risqué reputation since its creation.

⅓oz/1cl	grenadine
⅔oz/2cl	white sambuca
⅔oz/2cl	Irish cream liqueur

Pour each ingredient, in the order listed, over the back of a barspoon into a shot glass.

Sloe Comfortable Screw

When you talk about this drink, people think it's a joke. It isn't.

1oz/3cl	sloe gin
1oz/3cl	Southern Comfort
fresh	orange juice

Mix all ingredients in a mixing glass with ice. Strain into an old-fashioned glass with ice.

Spread Eagle

For moments like this, you need a reviving combination, and this recipe works.

½ oz/1.5cl	Irish cream liqueur
½ oz/1.5cl	Frangelico
½ oz/1.5cl	Remy Martin cognac
4 oz/12cl	hot coffee
2 oz/6cl	hot chocolate
	whipped cream

Build the ingredients in a heat-proof glass. Stir. Top with whipped cream.

Stiletto

You could definitely make a strong point with this earthy cocktail!

1⅔oz/5cl	bourbon
⅔oz/2cl	amaretto
⅔oz/2cl	fresh lime juice
garnish	a wedge of lime

Pour all ingredients into a shaker with ice. Shake. Strain into an old-fashioned glass filled with ice. Garnish with a wedge of lime.

Sweetheart

This is an aperitif with a delicate hint of bitter orange and sweet lemon.

1oz/3cl	vodka
1⅓oz/4cl	Aperol
⅔oz/2cl	limoncello (Italian liqueur)
⅔oz/2cl	fresh lemon juice
3⅓oz/10cl	cranberry juice
garnish	a stem of red currants and a sprig of mint

Put all ingredients into a shaker with ice. Shake. Strain into a highball filled with ice. Garnish with a stem of red currants on the rim of the glass beside a small sprig of mint.

Tie Me to the Bedpost

Created while in the throes of a fantasy, this is a creamy, sweet, and citrus-flavored cocktail for those long nights.

½oz/1.5cl	**Midori**
½oz/1.5cl	**lemon vodka**
½oz/1.5cl	**Malibu**
½oz/1.5cl	**fresh lemon juice**
2 dashes	**gomme syrup**

Shake all ingredients with ice. Strain into an old-fashioned glass filled with ice. Relish the moment.

Tuxedo

Berries and sugar with cachaça combine with the other ingredients to make this a formal-occasion cocktail.

2oz/6cl	**cachaça**
½oz/1.5cl	**Chambord liqueur**
1	**fresh lime, diced**
6	**raspberries**
3	**blackberries**
2 teaspoons	**brown sugar**

Muddle the berries with the lime and sugar in the bottom of an old-fashioned glass with a heavy base. Add the spirits and a scoop of crushed ice. Stir. Serve with a straw.

Vanilla Cognac

A very simple recipe that takes time to get the full flavor, but then, isn't romance like that, too?

2	**vanilla pods**
1 pint/½ liter	**cognac in a glass bottle**

Split the pods in half and add them to the cognac. Leave them to infuse the cognac with their flavor for about two weeks. Strain each measure into a small, tulip-shaped glass and serve after dinner to the one you love.

Velvet Rosa

All softness and light...this cocktail will appeal to your senses of sight and taste.

⅔oz/2cl	**white rum**
⅓oz/1cl	**peach schnapps**
1oz/3cl	**cranberry juice**
	champagne
garnish	**red rose petal**

Shake all ingredients, except champagne, with ice. Strain into a champagne flute and top up with champagne. Stir quickly to bring the effervescence into play. Garnish with a small, delicate red rose petal.

Venus

Full of citrus flavor, this cocktail combines the racy rum spirit with the freshness of the Italian aperitif Aperol.

1oz/3cl	**light rum**
½oz/1.5cl	**mandarin liqueur**
1oz/3cl	**fresh mandarin juice**
dash	**Aperol**
½oz/1.5cl	**fresh lime juice**
garnish	**orange spiral**

Shake all ingredients with ice. Strain into a chilled cocktail glass. Add the garnish.

Venus and Me

Fresh fruit juice and the flesh of figs combine to make this a cocktail fit for a goddess.

2oz/6cl	**vodka**
½oz/1.5cl	**Cointreau**
1oz/3cl	**guava juice**
½oz/1.5cl	**fresh lime juice**
2	**fresh figs, peeled and diced**
dash	**grenadine**
garnish	**slice of fig**

Muddle the figs with the lemon juice and grenadine until smooth. Pour into a shaker with ice and add the remaining ingredients. Shake. Strain into an old-fashioned glass filled with crushed ice. Add the garnish. Serve with a straw.

When Hal Met Sal

The ideal cocktail for those restaurant moments when you want some of whatever she's having!

1⅔oz/5cl	**chilled vodka**
2	**fresh, juicy figs**
½oz/1.5cl	**Cointreau**
1oz/3cl	**passion-fruit juice**
dash	**grenadine**
dash	**champagne**
garnish	**small fig wedge**

Scoop out the flesh from the figs and muddle in the bottom of the shaker. Add ice. Add the remaining ingredients, except champagne. Strain into a chilled champagne flute. Top up with champagne. Add a small fig wedge on the rim of the glass.

Whip Me Quick

More painful than Kiss Me Quick but probably much more fun!

1oz/3cl	**sweet vermouth**
1oz/3cl	**dry vermouth**
1oz/3cl	**brandy**
dash	**triple sec**
dash	**anisette**

Pour ingredients into a mixing glass filled with ice. Stir. Strain into a chilled cocktail glass.

Index

Acknowledgments

I'd like to thank all the beautiful women who have passed through the bar at

The Lanesborough for inspiring me to do this book. Thanks to Conny Jude, the

illustrator, who interpreted my concept of sexy women and sexy cocktails

brilliantly. Again, thanks to Sterling for going with the idea; to Lynn Bryan, and to

Fiona at Limelight Management.